Flower Arranging
from the Garden

A Wisley Handbook

Flower Arranging from the Garden

DAPHNE AND SID LOVE

Cassell

The Royal Horticultural Society

THE ROYAL HORTICULTURAL SOCIETY

Cassell Educational Limited
Villiers House, 41/47 Strand
London WC2N 5JE
for the Royal Horticultural Society

First published 1989
This edition 1992

British Library Cataloguing in Publication Data
Love, Daphne
  Flower arranging from the garden
  1. Ornamental flowering plants. Cultivation –
    Manuals
  – For flower arranging
  I. Title   II. Love, Sid
  6359′024745
  ISBN 0-304-32021-8

Photographs by Michael Warren, Michael Brockway,
Daphne and Sid Love
Line drawings by Graham Wall
Phototypeset by Chapterhouse, Formby
Printed in Hong Kong by Wing King Tong Co. Ltd.

Cover: a basket of late summer flowers and foliage
gathered fresh from the garden.
  Photograph by Michael Brockway
p.1: a fragrant arrangement including herb foliage, shrub
roses and dianthus.
  Photograph by Daphne and Sid Love
p.2: *Sisyrinchium striatum*, *Alchemilla mollis* and roses
make a pleasant composition in the garden – and in an
arrangement.
Back cover: an informal green and white spring
arrangement – hellebores, fritillaries, daffodils, *Stachyurus*
and *Acer*.
  Photograph by Daphne and Sid Love

Contents

Introduction   7

Techniques and equipment   8
  Conditioning   8
  Containers   10
  Mechanics   11
  Basic equipment   14

Summer pleasures, winter treasures   15
  Preserving   15
  Air drying   15
  Pressing   18
  Dessicants   18

A selection of plants   20
  Shrubs   20
  Climbers   35
  Roses   36
  Herbaceous plants   40
  Hardy annuals   56

Design in flower arranging   60

An arrangement of dessicant-dried flowers, including roses, delphiniums and hydrangeas

Introduction

When does a flower arranger become a gardener and vice versa? This is a difficult question to answer. Flower arrangers may begin gardening to grow the plants they cannot buy from a florist, only to find, having grown something wonderful, that they are loath to cut it and prefer to see it in the garden. Gardeners, on the other hand, are often so pleased with their efforts outside that they want to enjoy them in the house and so they become flower arrangers.

In this small book we hope to bring the two together harmoniously and to show how, with a little horticultural knowledge, you can successfully cultivate a garden that will supply you with plants for cutting all through the year, without spoiling the effect outside.

A summer arrangement (assymetrical triangle) in a Victorian cutlery box – gladioli, double petunias, garden pinks, Japanese anemones, butterfly antirrhinums, echinops and roses, with dried astilbe heads and varied foliage

Techniques and equipment

Flower arranging is a hobby to be enjoyed, not endured, and we will start by outlining one or two basic principles that will help you achieve this. First, we should explain the word material, which occurs throughout. This simply means any kind of flowers, foliage, berries and so on, whether fresh, dried or preserved, used in an arrangement.

CONDITIONING

Many people go into the garden on impulse, cut some flowers, bring them into the house and arrange them immediately. It is such a pity that they do not take a little extra care with preparing their flowers. This is what conditioning means – the preparation of your plant material before actually arranging it. It is, we suppose, the most important lesson to learn, for there is nothing more frustrating than to produce a beautiful arrangement which wilts a few hours later. Usually an overnight drink in deep, cold water will be sufficient, although some plants need more attention. However, we personally do not believe in "burning, bashing or boiling".

To condition your plants, begin by cutting the stems on the slant; this gives a larger surface area for water absorption (see figure 1). Remove any leaves that will come below the water level. With woody stems it is a good idea to cut a vertical slit 1 in. (2.5 cm) long up the stem. *Stems should always be re-cut immediately before placing them in the water*, even if you have only just gathered them from the garden or purchased them. Take the deepest bucket you have, preferably galvanized rather than plastic, because this keeps the water fresher and cooler, and with

(a)   (b)

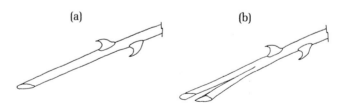

Figure 1: (a) cut stems on the slant for better water absorption; (b) cut a small vertical slit in woody stems

Hosta 'Thomas Hogg', a favourite with flower arrangers and an asset to any garden

side handles. Fill it with cold water and place in the coolest, darkest place available. Stand the plant material in the water and leave a minimum of six hours and, if possible, for 24 hours.

Some mature large leaves, such as those of hostas, benefit from being completely submerged in cold water for about six hours. Always remember to keep water off grey or downy foliage, otherwise it will become sodden and discoloured.

Most books suggest cutting flowers in the early morning or late evening, but we always cut in the middle of the day, especially in hot weather, since the material is usually flagging at this time of day and water is taken up readily, preventing airlocks from forming – one of the main reasons for premature wilting.

A few plants have a rather overpowering odour when brought into the home, for instance, flowering currants, *Ribes*, and the curry plant, *Helichrysum angustifolium*. If you add one teaspoon of liquid Savlon (the proprietary antiseptic) to every pint (0.5 litre) of cold water used for overnight conditioning, the odour will

The golden leaves of *Ribes sanguineum* 'Brocklebankii' are its chief attraction

disappear. This antiseptic solution can also be used to prolong the life of cut flowers, although there are of course many "long-lasting" products on the market for the same purpose.

Some plants, notably tulips and lupins, seem to have a mind of their own, twisting and turning and altering the overall shape of your arrangement. The remedy for this is starch. Mix one table-spoon of any cold water starch with one pint (0.5 litre) of cold water. Leave the material out of water until the stems become limp, then carefully wrap a few flowers at a time in newspaper to keep the stems straight, re-cut the stem ends and place in the starch solution. Allow the flowers to drink this liquid for approxi-mately six hours, remove them and put in a bucket of cold water overnight. After this treatment the flowers will not only stay in place in the arrangement, but will probably last three times longer.

CONTAINERS

Any type of receptacle may be used for arranging and it does not necessarily have to be a vase. When choosing a container, bear in mind the position it is likely to occupy and the colouring of the room, as well as the arrangement itself. If you find a container that is just the right shape but the wrong colour or with a hideous pattern on it, a pot of emulsion paint will work wonders; use a neutral colour or a shade to tone with your decor.

MECHANICS

Mechanics are the means by which plant material is held in the desired shape in the container and there are several types.

Wire mesh or chicken wire

This is one of the cheapest forms of mechanics. The best wire to use is 2 in. (5 cm) mesh, which is large enough to take the thickest stems. Cut a piece of wire mesh as wide as the container and approximately three times the depth, and remove the thick selvage at the edge. Roll the wire loosely into a tube and crumple it into the container, but do not push it too tightly together as this will make it difficult to insert the flower stems (see figure 2). If the mesh moves about, it can be secured with an elastic band around itself and the container, or it can be attached with adhesive tape, which can be cut and removed when the arrangement is finished.

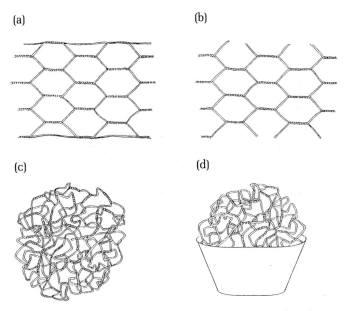

(a) (b)

(c) (d)

Figure 2: (a) wire mesh; (b) remove selvage; (c) roll loosely; (d) crumple into container

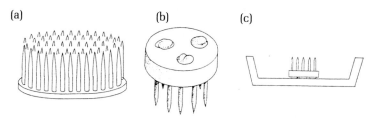

Figure 3: (a) pinholder; (b) place fixative on base; (c) press into position

Pinholders

Sometimes called kenzans, these are very useful for shallow containers or where the arrangement is not required to fill the whole container. They are quite expensive, but good ones should last a long time. It is sensible to buy the largest you can afford, because you can do a small arrangement on a large pinholder, but it is impossible to do a large arrangement on a small one.

Antique scales provide an unusual container for an all-the-year round arrangement, featuring houseplants, glycerined clematis seed heads and dried flowers

A midsummer arrangement (assymetrical triangle) in a box – New English roses, *Penstemon* 'Sour Grapes', *Lathyrus latifolius*, astrantias, astilbes and *Argyranthemum frutescens* 'Mary Wootton'

The pinholder consists of small vertical pins embedded in a lead base, which is often circular. The best type is heavy and has long pins set close together (see figure 3). It should be anchored firmly in the container with special fixative or plasticine. Make sure both pinholder and container are perfectly dry before fixing. Then place three small pellets of fixative or plasticine on the base of the pinholder, press it in position in the container and give a half turn, pushing downwards. Put a small cloth over the pins during the operation to protect your fingers.

Plastic foam

This water-retaining plastic is generally referred to as oasis, probably because this was the first brand manufactured. Very light when dry and usually green in colour, the foam comes in a variety of shapes, which can be easily cut to size with a kitchen knife. Cut the piece slightly smaller than the container, to enable you to top up with water when necessary. Submerge it before use in a bowl of water deeper than itself until it becomes heavy and sinks. The stems of your plants will then be held securely and can be inserted at any angle.

Once soaked, the foam should not be allowed to dry out and is best kept in a sealed plastic bag when not in use. It can be used several times until it becomes too full of holes.

If the foam needs anchoring, the simplest way is to tape across the top and on to the container. Alternatively, use a special foam anchor, of which there are two types available – the metal anchor, which is similar to a pinholder with longer, more widely spaced pins, and the cheaper plastic anchor, with four prongs. The anchor must be secured firmly in the container before use, fixing it in the same way as a pinholder (see p. 13), and the block of foam is then pressed on to it.

BASIC EQUIPMENT

A pair of floral scissors is essential. Unlike ordinary scissors, they cut cleanly so that flowers last longer; also they can cope with woody stems. The kind we use are very simple but effective, having short, stubby blades, with one side serrated, and a notch for cutting wire (see figure 4).

Other necessary equipment has already been described. In addition, you will require plastic sheeting to protect surfaces when working and, of course, your garden.

Figure 4: floral scissors

Summer pleasures, winter treasures

Even with the most careful planning, there is not always enough material available from the garden in the bleak months to make large arrangements for the home. With a little effort, you can easily turn "summer pleasures into winter treasures" by drying and preserving your favourite plants. Many flowers, seed pods and leaves are suitable, but the chosen material must be blemish-free, since every tiny imperfection shows up a hundredfold after preserving or drying. It is always best to gather it on a dry day.

PRESERVING

Foliage is the material most often used for preserving. First, condition it by giving it a deep, cold drink for 24 hours in a cool, dark place. Then make up the preserving solution, which consists of either one part glycerine to two parts boiling water, ensuring that the glycerine is completely dissolved, or one part anti-freeze to one part cold water. Stand the material in the solution, so that it reaches at least 2 in. (5 cm) up the stems, and top up with further solution as required. When the process is complete, the colouring changes evenly all over the leaf and at this stage the material should be removed immediately from the solution. Lay the preserved foliage on several layers of newspaper, leave for about a week to enable any excess solution to drain off and store wrapped in tissue paper in a cardboard box until required.

The length of time taken for preserving varies from plant to plant and from season to season, being anything from five days to six weeks or more. However, once preserved, the material will last indefinitely. A colour range from cream through tans and browns, dark greens and bluish grey can be expected.

The glycerine solution is slower to work than the anti-freeze, but gives more supple material. The anti-freeze solution tends to make the leaves a little brittle, but results in fascinating colour changes.

AIR DRYING

Air drying is used principally for flowers and seed heads. Always cut the material on a dry, warm day, when there will be a minimum of moisture on the plant surface. Pick only well formed, undamaged specimens and, as a general rule, choose flowers

15

An autumn arrangement (full triangle) of preserved material –
glycerined *Moluccella laevis*, *Atriplex* seed pods, *Alchemilla mollis* and
amaranthus; dried achillea, helichrysum and statice; and roses dried
in dessicant

which are just about to come into full bloom: blooms that are fully
open or have already begun to set seed will merely shed petals and
seeds when you attempt to dry them.

Remove the leaves from the stems, otherwise they will simply
wither and become trapped in the stems as they are drying. If the
flowers are fairly small, assemble them into small bunches and tie
them with string or plastic ties, leaving a loop to slide on a line or
hook. If the flowers are large, try to hang them separately, as they
are easily damaged if they have to be disentangled. The material
must be hung upside down so that the sap in the stems runs down
and prevents the necks from shrivelling before drying is
completed. Hang the bunches or individual flowers well apart, on
a line or on hooks in a cool, dry, airy place out of direct sunlight.
As the material dries it will tend to shrink, so you may need to
tighten the ties.

The length of time necessary for drying varies enormously. Delicate plants such as grasses may take only a week, but heavier flowers, containing more moisture, may need three weeks or more. Check the material to see if it feels dry and papery before taking it down, and store carefully in a box with a sheet of tissue on top. If flowers become crushed during storage, they can be gently shaken back into shape by holding them in steam.

Hydrangeas and the annual *Moluccella laevis* or bells of Ireland, which are very popular dried flowers, require a little extra attention. Pick the flowers, cutting hydrangeas on a stem of the current year's growth if possible, and strip off the leaves as usual. Stand the stems in about 2 in. (5 cm) of water and leave in a warm room until all the water has gone. The stems should then be tied, hung upside down and left to dry in the normal way.

An early spring arrangement (landscape) of daffodils, snowdrops and catkins, with glycerined box foliage and ivy seed pods at the base

PRESSING

Leaves, either single or in sprays, ferns, flat flowers and individual petals all press well. Pressing preserves the colour and prevents curling and shrivelling but, since it flattens the material, it is not suitable for very thick or succulent plants. Delicate flowers, leaves and petals should be placed between sheets of clean blotting paper and pressed in a flower press or inside a heavy book (see figure 5). Arrange the material carefully, to avoid creasing and rolled edges, and label each sheet. The longer the material is left, the better will be the colour retention when it is exposed to light. Six to nine months is advisable.

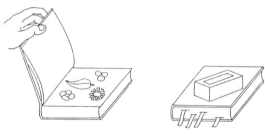

Figure 5: pressing in a book

Heavier foliage and ferns may be laid between sheets of newspaper under a carpet. Leave for a minimum of three weeks or until quite dry. Large flat leaves can also be ironed to speed up the drying process. Put them between sheets of newspaper and press firmly with a warm iron. The leaves may flop at first, but will stiffen as they dry. Place them under a carpet for a week to complete drying.

DESICCANTS

The practice of burying flowers in some form of desiccant, which absorbs moisture from them, has been known for a long time. There are three main types of desiccant – dry, fine silver sand; borax; and silica crystals. The first is rather slow and some flowers lose their colour before being properly dried out; the second comes in powder form and tends to stick to the petals, showing up particularly badly on darker flowers. We find by far the best medium is a silica product specially formulated for drying flowers. This consists of crystals with the texture of granulated sugar, which are bright blue when dry. Although completely harmless, they will absorb moisture from the hands and we recommend wearing rubber gloves or a barrier cream when handling them.

Roses and *Nigella damascena* preserve their colour perfectly when dried in dessicant

As before, the flowers should be perfectly dry when picked, choosing those which are in peak condition and fairly open. Cut the stems back to 2 in. (5 cm). Fill an airtight container with the crystals to a depth of about 2 in. (5 cm), lay the flowers in it (several can be dried at once) and gently cover them with the remaining crystals, taking care to separate each petal so that the desiccant enters every cavity. Put the lid on, making sure that the seal is airtight, and label with the contents and date.

Do not leave your flowers too long, or they will become over-dry and brittle. Examine them after two days by pouring off some of the crystals and, if you are satisfied that they are ready, tip the crystals into another box, leaving the flowers in the container. These can now be mounted on new stems, either binding them on to stub wires purchased from a florist with special stem tape, or glueing them on to dried stalks of grasses.

Finally, it is advisable to seal dried flowers to prevent them reabsorbing moisture from the air. The most effective method is to spray them with an aerosol of satin-finish polyurethane varnish, which gives an instant waterproof coating and helps to strengthen them. Two or three thin coats are better than one thick one.

After use, the crystals will have lost their bright blue colour and look like dirty sugar. Pour them into an old roasting tin and place in a fairly hot oven to dry out, when the colour will return. Let them cool off before returning to the airtight container, to be stored for re-use again and again and again.

A selection of plants

All the plants have been chosen primarily as good plants for the small garden, with the added bonus of being useful for flower arranging. Over the years we have grown them, they have proved their ability to produce worthwhile flowers and foliage and in some cases attractive seedpods. The majority are hardy and will succeed in any soil.

The descriptions of the plants include brief details of cultivation, information about any special conditioning or preserving requirements and advice on their uses in flower arranging.

SHRUBS

Shrubs are going to be the most permanent plants in your garden, so their selection requires some thought, particularly if you have room for only a limited number. They are especially valuable for foliage, both in the garden and in flower arranging, while evergreens can provide much appreciated material in winter.

Soil preparation is important and consists of thoroughly cultivating the site and adding humus in the form of well-rotted cow manure or compost. This should be carried out well in advance of planting, preferably from mid-September to October, so that planting can be accomplished from mid-November onwards, even into early March. Never plant in wet, soggy soil or in frozen ground. Do pay attention to the needs of the plant – whether it favours full sun or shade, acid or alkaline soil, well-drained or moist conditions, and remember to take its eventual dimensions into account when positioning. (For further information, see the Wisley Handbooks, *Shrubs for Small Gardens* and *Pruning Ornamental Shrubs*).

Many shrubs can be propagated from semi-ripe cuttings, taken from mid-August to the end of September and placed in a cold frame.

Abelia × grandiflora is one of our most attractive small shrubs, needing a protected site in full sun to get advantage of its beautiful colour. Semi-evergreen, it bears from July to September a mixture of pink and white flowers, with calyces in shades of purple which remain after the flowers. The hybrid A. 'Edward Goucher' has pink flowers. It grows to a height of 5 ft (1.5 m) and is happy in most soils except heavy clay. Prune in spring by removing any weak twiggy growths and one or two older stems.

Above: *Abelia* x *grandiflora* 'Edward Goucher'
Below: *Berberis thunbergii* 'Rose Glow'

The arching sprays give good outlines for autumn arrangements, going perfectly with the apricot shades of dahlias such as 'Shandy' or 'So Dainty'. Providing you condition the branches well and remove a few of the leaves, the lovely calices will last for weeks.

Berberis (barberry) is a valuable group of shrubs, many having beautiful flowers, others attractive fruits and foliage, although all have thorns as well. They thrive in any aspect and soil, but a little peat or leafmould added at planting will be beneficial. Allow plenty of room for them to develop into well-shaped plants. All grow about 4–5 ft (1.2–1.5 m) high. The following are deciduous.
B. koreana. Beautifully coloured leaves in autumn, with red oval berries.
B. × ottawensis 'Purpurea'. Deep purple foliage and yellow flowers followed by red berries.
B. thunbergii f. *atropurpurea*. Rich reddish purple leaves deepening in colour as winter approaches. In 'Rose Glow', the leaves of the young shoots are purple mottled with silver and pink, later becoming more intense. (See p. 21.)

If you can remove some of the thorns before arranging, to avoid tearing other plants, you will be pleased with the effect. The leaves do not last quite so long once they are into their autumn colours.

Buxus (box) are known by most people as hedge plants, but several are useful for the flower arranger. They are evergreen, tolerant of all soils, even very chalky conditions, and succeed in sun or shade. They may attain 10 ft (3 m) in height.
B. balearica. Bright green, leathery leaves.
B. sempervirens. 'Marginata' has green leaves with yellow margins. It tends to produce pure green shoots if growing too freely, which should be removed immediately they appear. 'Myrtifolia' has small narrow leaves which go a good bronze colour in winter.
B. wallichiana. Long narrow leaves.

If you leave your box plants unclipped, you will be able to use the large sprays of dainty foliage all through the year. Glycerine some for winter bouquets. Leave in the glycerine mixture for two weeks, remove, tie and hang in a cool dry place. After a few weeks they will be ready to use, having turned a wonderful cream shade.

Calluna vulgaris see *Erica.*

Chimonanthus praecox (winter sweet) is a deciduous shrub some 6–10 ft (1.8–3 m) tall. It is often grown in the open ground, but because it flowers in winter, we find that the best position is on a south-facing wall, where the blooms are protected from frost. These are pale lemon, waxy, with purple centres, and strongly perfumed. 'Grandiflorus' has deep yellow, reddish centred flowers. 'Luteus' has clear yellow flowers, appearing later, in February. They succeed in any well-drained soil, including chalk. When grown against a wall, pruning consists of the removal of the old flowered wood immediately after flowering. As the new shoots grow during the summer, tie them into their flowering positions, loosely enough to allow for the development of the stems.

Just a few sprigs of this delightful shrub will perfume the room, but remember to introduce them gradually into the heat of the home, otherwise the flowers will fall.

Cornus (dogwood, cornel) is a large genus of mainly deciduous shrubs and small trees. They will grow in any soil (except shallow chalk in the case of *C. kousa* var. *chinensis*) and in sun or partial shade. Apart from removing any odd crossing branches, no pruning is necessary.

The Cornelian cherry, *Cornus mas*

C. kousa var. *chinensis* (Chinese dogwood). A mass of white flowers, strictly bracts, covering the branches in June, creating a spectacular sight. As the flowers mature, they take on a pinkish tint and are followed by scarlet strawberry-like fruits in August. The leaves turn to beautiful bronze and crimson colours in autumn. Very slow growing after the first five years or so and, although it will eventually reach 20 ft (6 m), it will take many years to do so. Most gardens are enhanced by a small tree and we believe this to be one of the best, outstanding in an open position.
C. mas (Cornelian cherry). A large shrub or small tree about 10 ft (3 m) high, with dense twiggy branches, producing clusters of tiny yellow flowers before the leaves in February, followed by bright red berries, although these are not often seen in great numbers in the British Isles. The leaves turn reddish purple in autumn.

The Chinese dogwood lasts very well if you remove the foliage and, since there are usually so many flowers on the branches, it is better to remove one or two of these also. Arrange just a few branches and add some hosta leaves. The Cornelian cherry looks wonderful with a few daffodils or early forced tulips.

Danae racemosa (Alexandrian laurel) is an evergreen shrub with arching stems of shining lance-shaped leaves and bears tiny, green, insignificant flowers in the leaf axils and red berries in autumn. It grows to 3 ft (90 cm) and thrives in most soils, revelling in a moist shady place.

The foliage lasts a long time in water, needing only a deep drink to condition it. It is slow to glycerine, but worth the trouble, rewarding you with superb cream sprays.

Deutzia is a large genus of deciduous shrubs, growing well on almost any fertile well-drained soil. Most are in the height range of 4–6 ft (1.2–1.8 m) and flower in June and July. As they flower on wood made the previous year, all flowered wood should be pruned immediately flowering has finished, to encourage young growth from the base.

23

Deutzia gracilis (left) and *Erica cinerea* 'P. S. Patrick' (right)

D. elegantissima 'Rosealind'. Flowers of deep carmine pink.
D. gracilis. White flowers borne a little earlier than the others before the foliage has developed.
D. longifolia 'Veitchii'. Large clusters of lilac pink-tinted flowers.
D. purpurascens. White flowers tinted crimson and sweetly scented.
D. × rosea 'Venusta'. Large, white, bell-shaped flowers.

The branches make excellent background material for arrangements. Try sprays of *D. longifolia* 'Veitchii' with a few 'Lavender Lassie' roses and *Hosta* 'Halcyon' in a pewter teapot – they look spectacular. When using those which have fairly prolific foliage, remove one or two leaves before conditioning: the stems will last longer and the flowers show up better.

Elaeagnus are fast-growing evergreens (in the examples below) and do particularly well on the coast or in exposed areas. They make large shrubs of 10 ft (3 m) or more and bear tiny, white, highly perfumed flowers in autumn. They grow well in most fertile soils, but will not tolerate very shallow, chalky conditions.
E. × ebbingei. Large leaves with a silvery reverse.
E. macrophylla. Broad, dark green, rotund leaves.
E. pungens. 'Dicksonii' has deep yellow and green variegated leaves. 'Maculata' has splashes of gold on dark green. Remove any completely green-leaved shoots entirely with a knife.

These shrubs must be the most useful to the flower arranger, giving a constant supply of foliage throughout the year. On the dullest winter day, an arrangement using one of the golden forms will fill the room with sunshine. In summer try *E. pungens* 'Maculata' with yellow roses and some sprays of *Alchemilla mollis* in a brass container. All types can be glycerined. To retain some of the variegations, leave the stems in the solution for one week, remove, wrap carefully in newspaper and hang in a dark cool place until fully preserved. *E. × ebbingei* glycerines particularly well, giving a dark olive-green leaf surface and a pale cream underside.

Erica (heather) is a huge genus of evergreen shrubs which, with few exceptions, grow on acid soil. They will tolerate semi-shade but are at their best in open sunny positions. In spring they benefit from a top dressing of leafmould or peat to which a little general fertilizer has been added. Pruning is carried out immediately after flowering by clipping off the old flower heads. Listed below are just a few of our favourites out of the many suitable for flower arranging. The closely related *Calluna vulgaris* is also included here.

E. cinerea. 'Atrorubens' has long sprays of brilliant red flowers from June to September. 'Colligan Bridge' and 'P. S. Patrick' are bright purple. All grow up to 12 in. (30 cm).

E. herbacea (E. carnea). 'Cecilia M. Beale' is very free flowering, with white flowers on erect stems from January to March. 'Ruby Glow' has large, dark, rich red flowers in March and April and delightful bronze foliage. 'Winter Beauty' starts flowering in December, with lovely spikes of bright pink bells. All are at least 6–9 in. (15–23 cm) high and more wide.

E. vagans. 'Pyrenees Pink' has beautiful, long, pink flower sprays. 'St Keverne' is clear rose pink. About 20 in. (50 cm) tall.

Calluna vulgaris. 'Elsie Purnell' has spikes of silvery pink, double flowers, from deeper-coloured buds, in September to October. 'H. E. Beale' is one of the best for cutting, having very long racemes of rose-pink double flowers. 'Orange Queen' has magnificent gold foliage in spring, maturing to orange, and pink flowers. 'Serlei Aurea', with long sprays of white flowers from October to November, also has attractive golden foliage. All are up to about 2 ft (60 cm) high.

Elaeagnus pungens 'Maculata' in a late autumn arrangement, with ivy and chrysanthemums, dried cones, fungi and moss

Heathers last extremely well in water, requiring just a long overnight drink to condition them. They can be air dried, although they lose some of their colours. They can also be dried in desiccant, but do not leave them in crystals too long or they become brittle. The most successful method of drying is to use a potato. Select a large blemish-free potato and soak it for four hours in the Savlon solution. Cut the heathers, remove as much foliage as possible, insert the stems in the potato and put in a cool dark place. Leave undisturbed for two months and the flowers will be perfectly dried, without fading or shrinking.

Escallonia provides some of the most useful evergreen shrubs, flowering through the summer and into autumn. Mostly about 5–8 ft (1.5–2.5 m) high, they grow very well in mild coastal areas or in colder districts with wall protection. They thrive in all types of soil, providing it is well drained. Prune by cutting back the flowered growth immediately after flowering and removing any wayward branches. If a plant gets completely out of hand, it can be cut to within 3 in. (7.5 cm) in spring.

E. 'Apple Blossom'. Pink and white flowers in arching sprays in July and August. Rather slow-growing and excellent for the small garden.

E. 'Donard Brilliance'. Relatively large leaves and graceful branches covered with large, rich rose-red flowers.

E. 'Donard White'. Pink buds opening to white flowers over a long period, on a compact rounded shrub.

E. 'Langleyensis'. Arching branches wreathed in rose-pink flowers.

E. *macrantha*. Crimson-rose flowers and large, glossy, aromatic leaves. A taller species, this makes a good hedge plant for seaside gardens.

The arching sprays of escallonias are very useful in large arrangements and a few leaves should be removed to show the flowers at their best. The foliage and seed pods can be glycerined.

Euonymus is a popular and varied genus of hardy shrubs, which will grow in any soil, doing particularly well on chalk. Ornamental fruits and crimson scarlet foliage in autumn are the chief attractions of the deciduous kinds, while the evergreens have foliage in various shades of green, or variegated silver, yellow or golden. To get full advantage of the variegations, they should be planted in an open sunny position, though they will be quite successful in partial shade. Pruning for the deciduous types consists of removing twiggy growths and crossing branches. On the evergreens, cut back into the centre of the plant and remove any growths that spoil the shape.

E. *europaeus* 'Red Cascade'. A form of the spindle tree with good autumn colour and bunches of rosy red berries hanging from arching branches. Will reach a height of 10–12 ft (3–3.5 m).

E. *fortunei*. 'Emerald and Gold' is a variegated evergreen, with golden margins to the leaves turning orange and scarlet in winter. Quite short, to about 2 ft (60 cm). The slightly taller 'Emerald Gaiety' has white variegations, which become brilliant scarlet in frosty weather.

E. *japonicus* 'Ovatus Aureus'. Probably the best-known golden euonymus, with leaves edged in creamy yellow. Fairly slow growing and needs a sunny position to give of its best colour.

With spindle berries, it is best to remove all foliage to show off the fruits. Their warm pink colour goes well with pink dahlias and heads of metallic-looking hydrangeas. All the evergreen kinds condition well, although it is wise to wait until the leaves are mature before picking them. They are invaluable in winter, when they can be arranged with winter jasmine, *Jasminum nudiflorum*, and a few holly berries, or with hellebores and sprays of ivy berries. Do not be afraid to mix some of

Above: *Escallonia* 'Apple Blossom'
Below: *Euonymus fortunei* 'Emerald Gaiety'

the foliage with preserved material – for instance, creamy roses dried in desiccant. The leaves can be glycerined and sometimes the variegations will remain.

Fuchsia boasts many pretty flowering shrubs and a few of them, though not absolutely hardy, may be grown outside where they will survive all but extreme winters. They may be cut down to the ground by severe frosts, but will usually grow again in spring, especially if the dead stems are left on the plants to protect them over winter. Providing the soil is well drained, they will grow in any type, in sun or shade. Fuchsias flower continuously throughout summer and autumn and some have beautiful variegated foliage. All are deciduous and most grow to a height of roughly 4 ft (1.2 m).

F. 'Madame Cornelissen'. Large semi-double flowers of red and white.
F. magellanica var. gracilis. Abundant small scarlet and violet flowers on slender arching stems. 'Variegata' has green leaves with a creamy margin, flushed pink, and small scarlet and purple flowers. It needs winter protection in colder areas. The smaller spreading 'Versicolor' has leaves of grey green, flushed pink when young and developing creamy white markings when mature.
F. 'Mrs Popple'. Large scarlet and violet flowers over a long period.

It is a pity that fuchsias are not used more often in flower arranging. Many people think they do not last well in water, when in fact the contrary is true, as long as they have been conditioned well. We condition them overnight in the Savlon mixture. The lovely arching sprays are a great asset to summer bouquets. Stems of F. magellanica 'Versicolor' look good with the pink rose, 'Margaret Thatcher', and a few 'Pot Black' dahlias; we have a smoky pink, glass bowl which shows them off superbly. It is worth drying one or two small stems of variegated foliage in desiccant, as they are useful in small dried arrangements.

Helichrysum angustifolium (curry plant) is an evergreen sub-shrub about 2 ft (60 cm) high, with narrow, downy grey leaves, which give off a strong smell of curry. It produces heads of sulphur-yellow flowers in summer, but it is best to remove these at an early stage, which helps to preserve the greyness of the foliage. It needs a well-drained sunny position and benefits from a little shelter from cold winter winds. Although it can be left unpruned, better foliage is obtained if you cut back the previous year's growth in spring to within 2 in. (5 cm) of the base.

The curry plant is one of the daintiest grey foliage plants and the feathery sprays give good outline material in arrangements. The odour can be a little overpowering indoors, but an overnight drink in the Savlon solution will cure this. The plant can be air dried quite successfully, but we prefer to preserve it in glycerine, leaving it in the solution for about four days, then tying it in small bunches, hanging in a cool place and allowing it to dry out. Bunches of dried foliage can be placed in rooms that are shut up for any length of time and will keep them smelling sweet and fresh.

Ilex (holly) is a large and well-known genus of mainly evergreen shrubs. They will thrive in any soil and, it seems, in any position, making large shrubs about 10 ft (3 m) high after many years.

I. × altaclerensis. 'Belgica Aurea' ('Silver Sentinel', also known in gardens as I. perado 'Variegata') has large, rich green leaves fading to grey and edged with cream. 'Camelliifolia' has shiny, dark, almost spineless, camellia-like leaves, reddish purple when young, and large, deep red berries. 'Lawsoniana' has large, normally spineless leaves splashed with yellow in the centre. It tends to throw green shoots, which should be removed immediately.
I. aquifolium. 'Amber' is unusual for the large bronze-gold berries. 'J.C. Van Thol' has dark green, glossy, almost spineless leaves and generous crops of clear red berries.

Fuchsia magellanica 'Variegata' (left) and *Ilex aquifolium* 'J. C. Van Thol' (right)

Holly has some of the longest-lasting foliage, but it is somewhat particular in that it prefers shallow water. It is therefore very suitable for arranging in oasis. For Christmas decoration, we cut the branches two weeks in advance, place them in a bucket containing 6 in. (15 cm) water, to which has been added one tablespoon of Epsom salts, and leave in a sheltered position in the garden until required. The salts produce excellent foliage colour, and this method works well with most evergreens. The leaves may be glycerined, the best results being achieved in November, when beautiful rich mahogany shades are obtained. Holly does take a long time to preserve and it is essential to keep the container topped up with solution. *Ilex × altaclerensis* 'Belgica Aurea' is one of our favourite hollies. Arranged with yellow 'Graham Thomas' roses and a few stems of *Alchemilla mollis* in an old wooden box, it always creates a talking point with visitors.

Itea ilicifolia is a slightly tender evergreen shrub and in most areas is best suited by the protection of a wall. It will grow in partial shade or full sun, though care must be taken that the roots do not become dry. Its holly-like leaves are very attractive, with only a few spines, and green, faintly scented catkins 6 in. (15 cm) or more long are produced in late summer. It reaches about 9–10 ft (2.7–3 m).

This shrub is very useful for flower arranging and the catkins are especially good in large pedestal-type arrangements. The leaves can be glycerined, turning a lovely tan colour, and you can sometimes be successful with the catkins too.

Ligustrum lucidum, one of the privets, is a large evergreen shrub, 10 ft (3 m) or more high. 'Excelsior Superbum' is strikingly variegated, the leaves shaded deep yellow and creamy white. In 'Tricolor', the narrow leaves have a border of white and are tinged pink when young. White flowers are borne in autumn. They will flourish in any type of soil, in full sun or shade, although the variegations are more marked in an open position.

The foliage often remains on the plant throughout the winter and is excellent for arranging, whether you pick long sprays or just tiny side shoots. Condition in Savlon, if you dislike the odour, and do the same with the flowers, whose perfume can be a little overpowering.

Philadelphus (mock orange) are among our most popular deciduous shrubs and, although some are too rampant for the average garden, others are more restrained and can be recommended. The white, heavily scented flowers appear in June and July. They will grow in any type of soil and situation. Pruning should be carried out immediately after flowering, removing weak shoots and cutting back hard all flowered stems.

P. 'Belle Etoile'. Large white flowers with maroon centres, growing to about 6 ft (2 m) high.

P. coronarius. 'Aureus' is slightly taller than the preceding, with beautiful yellow young foliage and creamy white flowers. 'Variegatus' has crinkly leaves with a creamy white margin. Both should be planted in a position where they are shaded in the heat of the day, as the mid-day sun will scorch the leaves.

P. 'Erectus'. A profusion of rather small white flowers on an erect shrub 3–5 ft (90 cm–1.5 m) tall.

P. 'Sybille'. Of similar height, with arching branches carrying almost square, white, purple-stained flowers with an unusual orange scent.

Before conditioning sprays of philadelphus blossom, remove as many leaves as possible; this will make them last much longer. Get them into water immediately after cutting. During June, when there are many weddings, we have arranged huge bowls of mock orange, *Alchemilla mollis* and the wonderful peony, 'Snow Cloud', which is a very frilly double form. *Philadelphus coronarius* 'Aureus' is invaluable when you need bright golden material to lighten a dark corner. The best way to condition the foliage is in the Savlon mixture.

Philadelphus coronarius 'Aureus'

Photinia 'Red Robin' in a late spring arrangement (informal), with tulips, ornamental quince, ivy seed pods and bergenia leaves

Photinia × fraseri is the name for a group of hybrid evergreen shrubs, growing up to 10 ft (3 m) high and notable for their brilliantly coloured foliage. 'Birmingham' has pointed leaves of deep coppery red from spring into summer. In 'Red Robin', the bright red new shoots first appear in mid-February and continue to October. They will grow in most soils, including chalky ones, and prefer a sheltered position, especially in colder areas, as the young shoots appear early in the year and can be damaged by frost. No pruning is necessary except to remove badly placed branches.

These are among our favourite evergreens and it seems that the more you cut from them, the more they produce the beautifully coloured leaves. Condition in deep water. In very cold weather, it is essential to introduce the foliage gradually to the heat of the house. We condition it in the garage, then bring it into the cloakroom for a day and finally into the warmth of the lounge. Mature foliage can be glycerined.

Ribes (flowering currant) are hardy, spring-flowering, deciduous shrubs which will grow in all types of soil. Flowered and twiggy wood should be pruned hard immediately after flowering.
R. alpinum. Tiny greenish flowers followed by red berries on a densely twiggy bush some 5 ft (1.5 m) high. The hawthorn-like foliage turns various shades of rust and gold in autumn if growing in full sun, but it will tolerate shade.
R. odoratum. Loose racemes of yellow, beautifully scented flowers in April and black autumn berries. The shiny green leaves develop rich colours in autumn.
R. sanguineum. 'Brocklebankii' has pale pink flowers appearing about the same time as the golden leaves are beginning to unfurl. It requires a semi-shady position to prevent scorching the leaves. Reaches a height of 3 ft (90 cm). (See p. 10) 'King Edward VII' has deep crimson flowers and green leaves.

Above: *Spiraea nipponica* 'Snowmound'
Below: *Stachyurus praecox*

Flowering currants may be forced into flower after winter dormancy has broken. To do this, cut one or two branches in bud, place them in a bucket of Savlon solution, leave in a cool place in the home and spray twice a day with warm water. The flowers should open in about ten days, although the colour will be a little paler than normal. When conditioning naturally developed flowers and foliage, always add Savlon to the water, to remove the smell. Mature leaves can be glycerined.

Spiraea is a large and varied genus of deciduous shrubs, all of which grow happily in ordinary soil and a sunny site. Pruning, for those that flower before the end of June, is carried out immediately after flowering.
S. × arguta (bridal wreath). Profuse clusters of pure white flowers borne along the graceful slender stems in April and May, on a dense shrub some 5 ft (1.5 m) high.
S. nipponica 'Snowmound'. Small white flowers cover the long arching branches in June. Grows to 4–5 ft (1.2–1.5 m).
S. thunbergii. Of similar height, with white flowers produced in thick clusters along the slender downy stems in March and April.

The arching sprays of flowers are a delight to use, especially early in the year, when they can be arranged with white double tulips and a few leaves of Hosta undulata in a white container, giving a cool, crisp-looking arrangement. We always allow a few sprays to set seed before pruning, so that they can be glycerined. The leaves turn a gingery brown and the seed heads very dark brown; they are useful in dried arrangements.

Stachyurus is a small group of deciduous shrubs, of which only two are generally grown. Rather spreading in habit and about 5 ft (1.5 m) tall, they will grow well in all fertile soils, in full sun or partial shade. As the flowers appear early in the year, it is advisable to plant them where they will have some protection from frosts. Pruning is a matter of removing the odd old stem to encourage new growths immediately after flowering, but is not always necessary.
S. chinensis. Long racemes of pale yellow cup-shaped flowers, appearing at the end of February or beginning of March. The hazel-like green leaves give some attractive autumn colour.
S. praecox. Shorter trails of flowers, with larger leaves and stouter stems. In mild winters, it will flower as early as February.

Although the branches are somewhat stiff in appearance, they are a joy to use so early in the year, making you feel that spring is really on its way. Remember to bring them gradually into the heat of the home and they will last much longer. Just a few branches arranged on a pinholder in a shallow dish, with five or six daffodils and a little moss to cover the holder, will make a charming arrangement on a gloomy winter day.

Weigela are very attractive, easily grown, deciduous shrubs which thrive in any fertile soil, in a sunny position. They are first class for town gardens. The foxglove-like flowers are produced in May and June along stems grown the previous year, occasionally followed by a second flush of bloom in late summer. Pruning consists of thinning out and cutting back old flowering stems to within 2 in. (5 cm) of the old wood immediately after flowering.
W. 'Eva Rathke'. Long-lasting bright crimson flowers with straw-coloured anthers. Compact and rather slow growing, eventually to a height of 5 ft (1.5 m).
W. florida. 'Foliis Purpureis' is slow growing to about 3 ft (90 cm), with purple-flushed leaves contrasting well with the pink funnel-shaped flowers. The slightly taller 'Variegata' has leaves edged with creamy pink when young, maturing to gold, and pale pink flowers. (See p. 34.)

W. 'Looymansii Aurea'. An outstanding sight in spring and early summer, when the light golden foliage is enhanced by the pink flowers. Grows to about 6 ft (1.8 m) and is best planted where the leaves will have some shade from the mid-day sun.
W. 'Mont Blanc'. Large, white, fragrant flowers and vigorous growth.

Remove some of the foliage to reveal the flowers and they will last a long time if properly conditioned. The branches are useful in large groups and on their own. Select branches with an interesting shape, stand them in a tall pewter-coloured jug, place on a windowsill and let the light shine through them. In late summer it is worth glycerining the leaves, which give long arching sprays for winter arrangements.

CLIMBERS

Modern gardeners usually like to make use of every possible bit of space and we thought it might be helpful to include one or two climbers. Their trailing growths can be valuable for softening the edges of an arrangement and adding another dimension of interest.

Actinidia kolomikta is a slender deciduous climber to about 20 ft (6 m), with attractive tri-coloured leaves of creamy white, pink and green. It is easily grown in reasonable soil and is best against a sunny wall, to bring out the variegation of the foliage.

Clematis is a large and popular genus of climbers, mainly represented in gardens by the large-flowered hybrids. All prefer a sunny aspect and a cool, shady root run,

Opposite: *Weigela florida* 'Variegata'
Below: *Actinidia kolomikta*

in moist but well-drained soil. The species require very little pruning, apart from tidying up twiggy stems. (See also the Wisley Handbook, *Clematis*.)
C. cirrhosa var. *balearica*. An evergreen climber to about 10 ft (6 m), with attractive, finely cut leaves, which turn deep bronze in winter. Small, pale yellow flowers, spotted reddish purple within, are borne from September to March.
C. macropetala. Slender-stemmed deciduous climber to about 8 ft (2.5 m), having divided leaves and large violet-blue flowers with paler blue centres in May and June. These are followed by silky seed heads, which are well worth glycerining.

Hedera colchica 'Sulphur Heart' ('Paddy's Pride') is, we believe, one of the best ivies and it is completely hardy even in the coldest winters. The evergreen leaves are variable in both size and variegation, some being wholly green, some splashed with yellow and other entirely gold. It thrives in almost any situation and soil.

ROSES

One could write volumes about roses, but in this limited space we can only give a brief selection of those we have found useful in flower arranging. Roses need an open sunny site with good air circulation and will succeed in a wide range of soils, as long as they are not waterlogged. Large-flowered (hybrid tea) and cluster-flowered (floribunda) roses are usually grown in their own beds, though this is not essential. Feeding should be carried out at the end of March and again by the third week in July, certainly not later, using a balanced fertilizer. A top dressing of compost or well-rotted manure is also beneficial, applied when the soil is moist during the second half of April. Pruning is usually done in early March in the south and at the end of the month in the colder north. (For further information, see the Wisley Handbook, *Roses*.)

There are, of course, many roses suitable for arranging. It is a good idea to go round gardens and nurseries in July and again in September to see the different kinds in flower and check whether they are fairly disease-free. Remember too to choose colours that are going to be the most use to you: the softer colours are often more versatile than strident reds and oranges. We strongly recommend the following.

Large-flowered roses (hybrid teas)

'Asso di Cuori' ('Ace of Hearts'). Bright crimson-scarlet flowers on a par with florists' roses, very long lasting when cut. Sturdy upright growth, to 2½ ft (75 cm).
'Congratulations'. Lovely salmon-pink blooms on a strong grower, 4½ ft (1.3 m) high.
'Margaret Thatcher'. Beautiful porcelain or flamingo-pink flowers, lasting up to two weeks in water. Height about 3 ft (90 cm).
'Paradise'. Unusual silvery lavender blooms and dark glossy foliage. Height 3 ft (90 cm).
'Remember Me'. Freely produced, coppery orange blooms with a slight fragrance. Only 1½ ft (45 cm) high.

The large-flowered rose, 'Silver Jubilee'

'Silver Jubilee'. Large apricot-pink flowers over a long period. Very healthy. Height 2 ft (60 cm).

'Tynwald'. Large, creamy white, rather open flowers, having many petals. To 4 ft (1.2 m).

Cluster-flowered roses (floribundas)

'Amber Queen'. Fragrant, amber-yellow flowers. Height 2½ ft (75 cm).

'Anne Harkness'. Large trusses of apricot-orange flowers. Free flowering and long lasting as a cut flower. Height 4 ft (1.2 m).

'Bella Rosa' ('Toynbee Hall'). Very neat and free flowering, smothered in blooms of soft salmon pink. Height 2½ ft (75 cm).

'Brown Velvet'. Most unusual russet-brown blooms with reddish shading, which look really velvety. Definitely a flower arrangers' rose. Height 3 ft (90 cm).

'Korresia'. Golden yellow blooms of perfect shape with some fragrance. Height 3 ft (90 cm).

'Margaret Merril'. Beautifully scented, white flowers with a faint blush. Compact grower to a height of 3 ft (90 cm).

'Shocking Blue'. Very fragrant, deep magenta blooms with a hint of mauve, of hybrid tea shape. Height 3 ft (90 cm).

'Snowline' ('Edelweiss'). Lovely, centifolia-type, white flowers and sturdy growth. Height 2 ft (60 cm).

'Southampton'. Large clusters of shapely, soft apricot blooms with some perfume. Tall to 4 ft (1.2 m).

Climbers (all repeat flowering)

'Compassion'. Very fragrant, full-petalled flowers of light salmon shaded deep orange.

The New English rose, 'Graham Thomas'

'Dreaming Spires'. Golden yellow flowers with a distinct fragrance. Very vigorous grower.
'Handel'. Trusses of creamy white flowers, the edge of the petals suffused pink.
'Swan Lake'. Perfectly formed, large blooms, white tinted pink.

Patio roses

Known officially as dwarf cluster-flowered roses, patio roses are ideal for small gardens and for growing in ornamental containers.
'Sweet Dream'. Awarded Rose of the Year 1988. A bushy plant growing to a height of 1½ ft (45 cm), covered in masses of double, apricot-shaded blooms.

New English roses

Again, this is not a true classification, but the term for a group of roses produced by crossing modern varieties with some of the old garden roses. This gives you the best of both worlds – the wonderful perfumes and shapes of the old roses and the repeat flowering and neater habit of growth of modern roses. Most grow 4–5 ft (1.2–1.5 m) tall.
'Gertrude Jekyll'. An upright grower with very healthy foliage. The flowers are deeply scented, a perfect rosette of rich pink.
'Graham Thomas'. Cup-shaped, rich yellow flowers with a beautiful tea-rose scent.
'Mary Rose'. Delightful damask rose perfume, flowering very freely on sturdy, much branched stems in a lovely rich pink.

Roses are among the most valuable summer flowers for arranging and, if you take care to select good cutting kinds, they will last a very long time. It is essential to condition them well, getting them into deep cold water immediately after cutting. It is also a good idea to slit the stem for about 1 in. (2.5 cm) to provide a greater cut surface. Even with conditioning, some roses may flag and we find that the best cure is to give them a cold bath. Fill the bath with about 1 ft (30 cm) of cold water, submerge the heads as well as stems of the roses, re-cut them under the water and prick with a pin just under the head. Put newspaper over them to keep them under the water, leave for two hours, remove, wrap in fresh newspaper, place in a bucket of ice-cold water and leave overnight. Conditioned this way, they will last for several days.

If you have a ruby-coloured container, try arranging some 'Margaret Thatcher' roses with beetroot leaves and a few silky grey seed heads of clematis. This rose, with its thick leathery petals, dries well in desiccant. 'Brown Velvet' roses look extremely attractive in a mahogany box with epimedium foliage and dried seed heads of astilbe.

An arrangement of roses (round) – 'Brown Velvet', 'Sweet Dream', 'Remember Me' and the new 'Pink Pearl', with butterfly antirrhinums; no foliage is used apart from that of the roses

HERBACEOUS PLANTS

Many herbaceous plants are good for flower arranging, but in our small garden they really have to earn their keep: they should provide attractive flowers and/or foliage and if possible seed pods, and also be suitable for using both fresh and dried or preserved.

Thorough preparation of the soil (see p. 20) is just as important for perennials as for shrubs and they are best planted in early autumn or, particularly in the case of summer- and autumn-flowering plants, in spring. These are also the times to divide herbaceous plants, which is necessary every few years when the clumps become overcrowded. For the majority, division is the simplest method of propagation.

Achillea (yarrow) ranges from tiny alpines to large border plants. They relish the sun and will thrive in most soils, although preferring alkaline conditions. All have flat, dense heads of flowers in summer and autumn. 'Coronation Gold' and similar types prefer to be left undisturbed for at least three years.
A. 'Coronation Gold'. Yellow flowers on stiff 3 ft (90 cm) stems and fern-like foliage.
A. 'Moonshine'. Pale yellow flowers and soft grey, feathery foliage. To 2 ft (60 cm).
A. *ptarmica* 'The Pearl'. Large clustered heads of double button flowers and shiny green, pointed leaves. Height 1½ ft (45 cm).

In addition to these, there are now many beautiful orange, peach and red achilleas available. All are long lasting as cut flowers and will dry successfully just as they are. However, better colour is obtained if you carefully wrap individual heads in newspaper and hang to dry in the normal way.

Aconitum napellus (monkshood) is characterized by beautiful spikes of helmet-shaped flowers and dark green, finely cut foliage. It prefers moist soil in partial shade, but will grow quite happily among other border plants. The roots are poisonous and should be handled with care. 'Bicolor' has flowers bicoloured blue and white in late summer and grows 3–4 ft (90 cm – 1.2 m). 'Newry Blue' has deep blue flowers. 'Ivorine' is about half the height and produces small creamy white flowers in spring.

Cut flowers should be conditioned in the Savlon mixture. Flower spikes can be air dried successfully, if cut before they are fully mature, and the foliage is worth glycerining.

Alchemilla mollis (lady's mantle) is one of the most sought-after plants by the flower arranger. Clouds of airy, greenish yellow flowers are held on stiff 1–1½ ft (30–45 cm) stems in summer, above the beautifully shaped, downy, greyish green leaves, which look like jade fans when just unfurling. To enjoy the plant at its best, it should be planted in a moist shady position, where the flowers will last longer and retain their fresh green colour. It self-seeds readily, although cutting will help to curb it. (See p. 2.)

This makes a perfect foil for other flowers, but also looks good arranged with just a few epimedium leaves. The flowers will air dry very well, keeping their colour. They can also be glycerined, turning pale olive green, as can the leaves.

Achillea 'The Beacon'

Anemone × hybrida (Japanese anemone) is the well-known *A. japonica* of gardens, with large, clear carmine-pink flowers in late summer and autumn and vine-like leaves clothing the stems. There are many forms with flowers in different colours, mostly growing 4–5 ft (1.2–1.5 m) tall, but some a little shorter. They include 'Louise Uhing', with pure white semi-double flowers and golden stamens; 'Max Vogel', with semi-double rosy pink flowers; and 'September Charm', with very large, pink flowers. They will grow in sun or partial shade, in any good soil.

Japanese anemones are long-lasting cut flowers, provided they are conditioned well and the stems are re-cut before putting in the Savlon solution. You can try glycerining some stems of foliage, which should turn a good amber colour, although it does not always work. Flower heads can be dried in desiccant, but it is advisable to wire the stems first.

Aquilegia (columbine) contains some excellent garden plants, all with the distinctive, spurred, nodding flowers in summer. Once established, they seed freely and they will grow in any type of soil. However, the flowers last longer if there is some dappled shade during the hottest part of the day. Propagate by seed.
A. vulgaris (granny's bonnet). Flowers in various shade of blue, purple or white, single or double, carried on stiff 1½ ft (45 cm) stems. There are many hybrid groups, notably the long-spurred hybrids, available in a wide range of colours and growing to 2 ft (60 cm) tall. The Fairyland group have large heads of flowers on sturdy 1 ft (30 cm) stems. They are hardy perennials which may be raised from seed sown in February to flower in July and will continue for several years, often seeding themselves. (See p. 42.)
A. 'Norah Barlow'. Double, pinkish green flowers, deepening as they mature, and blue-grey, deeply cut foliage. Height 4 ft (1.2 cm).

The flowers are long lasting in water if you pick them when they are just beginning to show colour. The large blue-grey leaves of some kinds are also useful in blue and

41

Above: mixed aquilegias
Below: *Baptisia australis*

pink arrangements. Glycerined seed pods look good in winter arrangements and the flower heads can be dried in desiccant.

Aster ericoides (heath aster) and its forms are not so widely known as the larger-flowered Michaelmas daisies, but they compensate for the tiny individual florets by having fuller sprays of flowers, produced from August to September. They grow 2½–3 ft (75–90 cm) tall and will succeed in almost any situation, including poor dry soils. They usually need splitting after three or four years. Among the forms are 'Brimstone', with arching sprays of sulphur-yellow flowers; 'Delight', with graceful sprays of minute, white, gold-centred flowers; 'Ringdove', with pretty, little, rosy lavender flowers; and 'White Heather', with sprays of tiny, star-like, white flowers.

Pick the sprays of flowers just as they are beginning to show colour, condition them in the Savlon solution and they will last a long time in arrangements. They can sometimes be air dried successfully and small, side flowering shoots can be dried in desiccant.

Baptisia australis is a fine herbaceous plant with dainty, soft blue-grey foliage and deep blue, pea-like flowers borne on rigid stems in early summer, followed by pea-like seed pods. It reaches a height of about 3 ft (90 cm) and will grow in any fertile garden soil, preferring a sunny position.

Small side pieces of foliage can be used in medium-sized arrangements and whole stems are useful in large pedestals. It is better to wait until the foliage is mature before cutting, then condition it in water to which a little Savlon has been added. The foliage can be pressed, retaining its grey colour, or it can be preserved in glycerine. Leave the stems in this solution for only one week, remove, tie in small bunches and hang in a cool dark place for four weeks, when the leaves will turn an attractive black. The pure blue flowers are invaluable in summer arrangements, when there is a shortage of this colour. Condition as for the leaves. Smaller flower spikes can be air dried, although the best method is to dry them in desiccant. The seed pods will dry on the plant and turn black, before bursting open and twisting into interesting shapes. We prefer to glycerine them as soon as the seed is set, so that the pods become black but remain closed.

Bergenia (elephant's ears) is a group of plants with thick leathery, evergreen leaves, fleshy rootstocks and flowers in various shades of pink or white. Although they will grow in most soils, they prefer a rather light acid soil and generally do best in light shade. As they come into flower from March onwards, some protection from shrubs or trees will ensure they do not get damaged by later frosts. A mulch of well-decayed leafmould in spring is also beneficial. They make excellent ground-cover plants, mostly growing about 1 ft (30 cm) high.
B. 'Ballawley'. Leaves turning reddish bronze during cold weather and sprays of pale pink, green-eyed flowers, which in some seasons dry perfectly on the plant.
B. cordifolia. Leathery, rounded leaves becoming scarlet in winter and spikes of deep pink flowers. (See p. 44.)
B. crassifolia. Very fleshy spoon-shaped leaves and branching panicles of large, almost red flowers.
B. purpurescens. Smaller oval leaves and purplish pink flowers. Grows only 9 in. (23 cm) tall.

The leaves are excellent for flower arranging. They give visual weight to any design and have the bonus of being available for almost 52 weeks of the year. The flowers can be dried in desiccant or air dried.

Bergenia cordifolia (left) and the Korean chrysanthemum, 'Grandchild' (right)

Campanula persicifolia (bellflower) bears spikes 3 ft (90 cm) or more tall of beautiful, blue, cup-shaped flowers appearing continuously throughout the summer. 'Blue Belle' and 'Telham Beauty' have larger flowers and 'Snowdrift' is a white form. They thrive in most types of soil, in sun or partial shade.

The flowers are easy to condition and long lasting. Remove each bloom as it fades to allow the remaining buds to open. Smaller flower spikes may be dried in desiccant.

Chrysanthemum Korean hybrids are now enjoying a well-deserved revival. They are true hardy perennials and tolerant of most soils, but they do require some humus incorporated in the soil when preparing the site. The roots should not be allowed to become too wet in winter and, if your soil tends to be waterlogged, it is a good idea to mix in a little pea shingle or peat for drainage. In most cases the plants will need staking. If you leave them in the open ground all winter, they are best dug up in spring and split into smaller plants for replanting elsewhere in the garden, since they like fresh positions each year. By careful selection of hybrids, it is possible to have them in flower from late July until early November, even longer if the weather is kind. Not only do these chysanths have a long flowering season, but they exhibit a great variety of flower colours and types, from single to fully double and with spoon-shaped, quill-like or flat petals. We recommend a few of the hybrids available, mainly those that we use most:

'Copper Nob', glowing copper, semi-double, October to November, 2 ft (60 cm). 'Daphne', salmon-pink, single September to October, 2½ ft (75 cm). 'Grandchild', lilac mauve, double, September, 1½ ft (45 cm). 'Irene', smoky pink, single spoon type, August to September, 2 ft (60 cm). 'Louise', apricot spoon type, September, 2 ft (60 cm). 'Marion', glowing chestnut red, spoon type with anemone centre, August to September, 2½ ft (75 cm). 'Mary', cream, single, very long stems, September to October, 2½ ft (75 cm). 'Starlet', honey-coloured, single, spoon type, August to September, 2 ft (60 cm). 'White Gloss', white, semi-double, spoon type, August, 2 ft (60 cm).

The flowers last very well if conditioned in the Savlon mixture. The quilled types are comparable to those sold in flower shops.

Cimicifuga racemosa (bugbane) is a striking plant with tall spikes of tassel-like, creamy white flowers, slightly fragrant, rising above leathery, deeply cut, toothed leaves in summer. Although reaching heights of up to 6 ft (1.8 m), the stems are very strong and seldom need staking. It enjoys partial shade and moist soil, but will tolerate full sun if grown among other plants to keep the roots cool.

Both leaves and flowers are useful for arrangements, needing only an overnight drink of cold water. The leaves can be glycerined and turn a good olive green. If they wither in the solution, wait for two weeks and try another batch; each year they seem to vary in the time they are ready for successful preserving and it is a matter of trial and error. Let some flower spikes go to seed and then either allow them to dry on the plant, or cut them and leave in the glycerine or anti-freeze preserving solution for one week, tie and hang upside down and allow to dry in the normal manner.

Crocosmia contains several late summer- and autumn-flowering plants with branching stems of small lily-like flowers and magnificent sword-shaped leaves. They will grow in sun or partial shade, in any well-drained soil. Some are not reliably hardy and it is advisable to plant them at the foot of a south-facing wall. They increase readily from corms and need dividing after three years to ensure the best effect.
C. × crocosmiiflora. 'Citronella' has lemon-yellow flowers on 2 ft (60 cm) spikes. 'Star of the East' has pale orange-yellow flowers.
C. masonorum. The hardiest, with arched sprays of large, orange-scarlet flowers, some 2½ ft (75 cm) high.

The sword-shaped leaves are good for giving height and emphasis to arrangements. They glycerine well, turning a rich brown, and can also be pressed. The arching flower stems are ideal outline material and can sometimes be air dried successfully. If a flower spike is allowed to set seed, it is best to air dry it, when the pea-size seeds turn bright orange, keeping their colour throughout the winter. Glycerining results in a tan-coloured spike.

Cimicifuga simplex 'Elstead Variety' (left) and the garden pink, 'Joy' (right)

Dianthus is the source of two much-loved plants, the carnation and the pink. Garden pinks need a sunny position and do better in alkaline soil. In acid conditions, it is a good idea to add some limestone. They are best planted during September and October, so that they can become established before severe winter weather occurs. There is, of course, a tremendous range of colours and forms, all fragrant and about 1 ft (30 cm) high, mostly flowering from May to August. They include 'Dad's Favourite', having white flowers with a chocolate edging to the petals; 'Inchmery', with semi-double, pale pink flowers; 'Joy', with cerise-pink flowers (see p. 45); and 'Musgrave's White', with white flowers with a green eye.

Very long lasting as cut flowers, pinks look beautiful arranged by themselves with their own greyish green foliage; just a few stems will perfume the whole room. The few-petalled kinds dry well in desiccants and, if they are strong smelling, retain their perfume.

Dictamnus albus (burning bush) is an excellent plant with vigorous thong-like roots. These resent disturbance and it should be left to become established. The dark green, divided, leathery leaves give off a lemon fragrance when rubbed and the scented white flowers, with unusually long stamens, appear in early summer, followed by star-shaped seed pods. It grows to about $2\frac{1}{2}$ ft (75 cm). The slightly taller var. *purpureus* has flowers of soft pink veined with purple, but may not come true from seed. They require a sunny spot in any well-drained soil.

All parts of the flower are useful for arranging and the flowers and foliage can be used fresh. The flowers can be dried in desiccant and the leaves can be glycerined around mid-July, turning a lovely deep cream. The seed pods can be air dried or glycerined as soon as mature.

Echinops (globe thistle) grow in any soil, but they are best in full sun and dislike root disturbance. Some grow very tall and the shorter ones will look more balanced in the average small garden. They have spiny, jagged, grey-green leaves, stiff grey stems and prickly, round flower heads in late summer.
E. niveus. Unusual white flowers, $3\frac{1}{4}$ ft (1 m) high.
E. ritro. 'Blue' has clear blue globes, 3 ft (90 cm) high. 'Taplow Blue' has spectacular, steely blue heads and grows to 5 ft (1.5 m). The slightly smaller 'Veitch's Blue' is a bright deep blue.

These long-lasting cut flowers will dry very well in an arrangement. However, to obtain the best dried heads with the brightest colours, you should pick them as soon as the flowers start to show colour, hang them upside down wrapped in newspaper, to exclude any light, and leave for about two months before unwrapping.

Epimedium are useful ground-cover plants, preferring a cool shady position but also thriving in a sunny place, providing the soil does not dry out. Although the spring flowers are delicate and attractive, it is for their evergreen foliage that we grow them. The young leaves are pale green and prettily veined in spring, gradually deepening as they mature, and in autumn they develop beautiful shades of bronze and deep scarlet, becoming more vibrant as the weather turns really cold. They are in the height range 9–12 in. (23–30 cm).
E. alpinum. Rosy purple flowers and shiny green leaves.
E. pinnatum. Bright yellow flowers and deeply cut leaves.
E. × versicolor 'Sulphureum'. Pendulous pale lemon flowers and spiny-toothed leaves which are a magnificent red when young.

The flowers of epimediums are best enjoyed on the plants, as there is no foolproof way of conditioning them after cutting. However, they can be dried successfully in

Above: burning bush, *Dictamnus albus*, and var. *purpureus*
Below: *Echinops ritro* 'Veitch's Blue'

Euphorbia griffithii 'Fireglow'

desiccant, even if the results are very fragile. Young leaves are too thin to condition, although the starch method should prolong their life a little. It is best to wait until the middle of July before cutting the foliage. If the leaves have not coloured sufficiently in winter, cut a few stems, tie them in a bunch and lay them under a hedge for two or three days, where the weather will work on them and sharpen up the colour. There is no need to put them in water for these few days and they can then be used in the normal way. In August it is worth preserving a few leaf sprays in glycerine or anti-freeze, when they will turn a deep olive green.

Euphorbia (spurge) is a very large genus whose distinguishing feature is the conspicuous bracts surrounding the insignificant flowers. They will grow in any soil and are equally happy in full sun or partial shade.
E. griffithii 'Fireglow'. Orange-red bracts in early summer, later green, on 2½ ft (75 cm) stems. The spreading roots are rather invasive, but offending shoots can be easily severed with a spade.
E. polychroma. Bright gold bracts in spring, fading to green, on 1 ft (30 cm) stems.
E. robbiae. Pale yellow-green bracts in summer, turning to various shades of rust as they age, above rosettes of dark evergreen leaves. Height 2 ft (60 cm). Try to plant some in full sun and some in semi-shade; this will give you a longer flowering period.

The lime-green colouring of spurges combines well with most flowers. A word of warning, however: do be careful of the white milky sap exuded by the stem when cut, as it can cause skin irritation. It is advisable to cut only mature stems and to condition them in the Savlon mixture. *Euphorbia robbiae* may be air dried.

Heuchera are attractive herbaceous plants for the border or rock garden. They are happy in sun or some shade and will tolerate most soils, though they do not give their best performance in heavy clay. The rounded hairy leaves are evergreen and

48

turn excellent colours during autumn and winter, while graceful, tiny bell-shaped flowers are held on slender stems in early summer, often continuing into autumn. They grow 1½–2 ft (45–60 cm) high. As the plants tend to raise themselves above soil level, mulch them in early spring with well-rotted compost, leaf mould or peat, plus a little general fertilizer. This will also help to prolong the flowering period. The roots should not be disturbed too often and division about every three to four years, according to growth, should be sufficient.

H. micrantha. Creamy white, frothy flowers.

H. sanguinea (coral bells). Large flowers in shades of pink through to crimson, depending on form. 'Scintillation' is bright pink; 'Red Spangles' is deep red.

The airy sprays of flowers look wonderful mixed with other summer plants. Condition fresh flowers and leaves in deep cold water. Dry some of the coloured foliage in desiccant; it is useful for giving visual weight to smaller arrangements.

× **Heucherella** are hybrids between *Heuchera* and *Tiarella*. They have similar evergreen foliage, beautifully lobed and sometimes marbled, and dainty sprays of bell-shaped flowers.

Hosta (plantain lily) is an increasingly popular group of plants, hardy, easily grown and thriving in dense or partial shade or in sun. Hostas do well in ordinary garden soil, but they benefit from a top dressing of well-rotted cow manure, garden compost, leafmould or peat, to keep the soil cool and moist – conditions in which they revel. The bold foliage is their main feature and there is great variety in shape, colour, size and texture. The spikes of lily-like flowers, white, lilac or violet, are produced mostly in summer. If you have problems with rabbits, keep a close watch

Heuchera sanguinea 'Red Spangles'

Kniphofia 'Little Maid'

for them in spring, when they can cause much damage to the new shoots. Slugs can also be a nuisance. The following are a few of our favourite hostas.

H. *crispula*. Large, wavy-edged leaves with white margins and violet flowers, growing to 2 ft (60 cm) tall.

H. 'Halcyon'. Deeply ribbed, grey-green, small leaves and pale lilac flower spikes. Height 1 ft (30 cm).

H. *plantaginea* var. *grandiflora*. Pale green, oval leaves and spikes of large, white, trumpet-shaped flowers, beautifully scented, up to 3 ft (90 cm). Will grow in a warm position.

H. 'Thomas Hogg'. Dark green leaves edged with white and lavender flowers, to 1½ ft (45 cm). (See p. 9.)

H. *tokudama*. Unusul ribbed leaves with green, blue and pale gold merging in various patterns. Flowers mid-lavender, 2 ft (60 cm) high.

H. *undulata*. Small undulating leaves, green with irregular yellow markings, and pale lavender flowers, to 1½ ft (45 cm).

Hostas are much sought after by flower arrangers for the leaves. These condition well by the deep water method, except when very young. Submerge young leaves in cold water for one hour, then let them drink in a bucket overnight, remove and place in a polythene bag, seal tightly and leave in a cool dark place for two days, after which they will become very crisp and will be ready for use. To dry the foliage, cut it in late summer when it feels leathery, put into a container of 3 in. (7.5 cm) of water, place in a dark warm position and leave for a month. Once it is dry, take out of the container and store until required. You will find the leaves have twisted into wonderful shapes, but use them with care as they are a little brittle. The seed pods can be either air dried or glycerined. The fresh flower spikes look well in arrangements, especially with pink and mauve flowers.

Kniphofia (red hot poker) has given rise to numerous striking hybrids which, if chosen carefully, can be had in flower throughout summer and autumn. They need a sunny spot in fairly rich, well-drained soil and are mostly in the range of 3 ft (90 cm) high. Remove faded flower spikes immediately to encourage a longer flowering period. Our personal selection includes 'Bees Sunset', with gold, scarlet-tipped flowers; 'Little Maid', with pale lemon flowers; 'Maid of Orleans', with creamy white flowers; and 'Slim Coral', which has coral flowers with very thin stems.

Condition the flowers with the starch solution.

Lathyrus latifolius (perennial pea) is a free-flowering climber 2–8 ft (60 cm – 2.4 m) high. It is best trained on a fence and may need some tying in to keep it in order. It requires sun and well-drained soil. The sprays of lovely pea-like flowers, in white, lavender, pink or purple, appear in summer, and there is also a pretty apricot form. It may be propagated by seed sown in gentle heat from October to February, or in a cold frame from February to April.

The perennial pea is long lasting as a cut flower and even the flowerless trails are attractive in arrangements. When the seeds have set and the leaves are mature, try glycerining some sprays. The flowers may also be dried in desiccant.

Phlox paniculata forms are some of the finest herbaceous perennials, lightly perfumed and available in a great many colours. They prefer rich soil, on the heavy side, with a good supply of well-rotted cow manure. On lighter soil, they tend to suffer from dryness at the roots, unless watered well in hot weather, or alternatively, planted in semi-shade. Eelworm can be a destructive pest with phlox,

51

resulting in contorted growth, curling of the leaves and yellowing or withering of the flowering shoots. Plants attacked by eelworm must be burnt. Root cuttings taken in autumn, inserted in boxes of sandy soil and placed in a cold frame, are the only method of propagation to avoid the spread of eelworm.

The large pyramid-shaped heads of flowers are borne in summer and they grow about 3–4 ft (90 cm – 1.2 m) tall. Among recommended forms are 'Admiral', with white flowers; 'Brigadier', with salmon-scarlet flowers; 'Chintz', having pink flowers with a red eye; 'Le Mahdi', with deep violet-blue flowers suffused with white; and 'Mother of Pearl', which has white flowers flushed pink.

Providing the flowers are conditioned well, they are long lasting in arrangements. Always get the stems into water immediately after cutting, because once they have wilted they seldom recover. It is a good idea to remove some of the foliage too. Check the arrangement regularly and remove any dead flower heads, to enable the buds to continue opening and keep your design looking crisp. A large group of phlox will fill the air with their delicate perfume. We also like to mix them with old English roses. Small heads of flowers can be dried in desiccant.

Phygelius are technically shrubs in warmer regions, but they perform well as herbaceous border plants which die down in winter. Plant in full sun in any type of soil, in the open or against a wall. It is advisable to give them a sheltered position in cold areas. They produce tubular flowers throughout summer and autumn and grow some 3 ft (90 cm) high.
P. aequalis 'Yellow Trumpet' and the hybrid 'Moonraker' have pale, creamy yellow flowers.
P. capensis 'Coccineus'. Abundant orange-scarlet flowers.

Condition flowers for fresh arrangements in the Savlon solution. Allow some flower spikes to set seed as these glycerine well and can also be air dried.

Polygonatum × hybridum (Solomon's seal), a hybrid of a native British species, is the plant usually grown in gardens. It loves moist, shady conditions. The hanging bell-shaped flowers, white marked with green and slightly fragrant, are carried on graceful, arching stems in May and June, together with broad green leaves. It grows to 2–3 ft (60–90 cm). There is also a variegated form, which is not so vigorous but worth finding space for. An annoying pest is sawfly caterpillar, which skeletonizes the leaves at a rapid rate. However, spraying or dusting with malathion at the first sign of damage will soon solve the problem.

The foliage is very useful for giving dramatic outlines to spring arrangements. It can be preserved in glycerine or anti-freeze, but leave in the solution for one week only as the leaves quickly become saturated and limp, then remove, wrap carefully in newspaper to absorb any surplus solution, tie and hang upside down to dry in the normal manner; the leaves turn very pale cream. When using the flowering stems, take off one or two leaves to lighten the effect.

Rudbeckia (cone flower) are very tolerant plants, thriving in any open sunny situation and doing well in heavy soils. They will need a little support, especially in wet summers. The daisy flowers appear in late summer.
R. laciniata. Golden yellow flowers with conical green centres and dark green leaves, unevenly divided into deeply cut segments. Height 5–8 ft (1.5–2.4 m).
R. nitida 'Goldquelle'. Beautiful double form with golden yellow, greenish-centred flowers and slightly lobed leaves, 2½ ft (75 cm) tall.

Rudbeckias are excellent cut flowers. Allow some seed heads to form, as they glycerine well. Flower heads can be air dried or dried in desiccant.

Above: *Phlox paniculata* 'Brigadier'
Below: *Phygelius aequalis* 'Yellow Trumpet'

Solidago 'Crown of Rays'

Sisyrinchium striatum prefers a sunny open position, although it will tolerate partial shade. A well-drained soil is essential, with some leafmould or peat added when planting. The 2 ft (60 cm) spikes of small, creamy white flowers appear above tufts of grey-green, iris-like leaves in summer. It is a good idea to remove any dead leaves as they appear, which helps to keep the crown dry. The plants are sometimes shortlived, but they are easily increased by root division in autumn and the seed will germinate freely if allowed to drop to the soil. Transplant the resultant seedlings into pots when large enough to handle, grow on to become established, then replant into the open ground. (See p. 2.)

The flowers will last up to six weeks when cut, although you have to take the trouble to remove the individual flowers as they die, so that all the buds will continue to open. Allow some spikes of flower to set seed and glycerine them for winter arrangements.

Solidago (golden rod) will grow in any soil in an open sunny position or in semi-shade. The newer hybrids are generally shorter growing, 2–2½ ft (60–75 cm), and not so rampant, flowering in late summer. 'Crown of Rays' has mustard-yellow, rather flat-headed flowers. 'Lemore' has flowers of soft primrose yellow.

The flowers are long lasting and good for filling in large arrangements. They can be air dried or small pieces of the flower heads can be dried in desiccant.

Stachys macrantha (betony) will grow in most soils, except heavy clay, in full sun or light shade. The heart-shaped, crinkly, hairy foliage makes a good foil for the whorls of purple-violet flowers on erect 1 ft (30 cm) spikes in May. 'Superba' has flowers of deeper purple-violet. 'Superba Rosea' has larger flowers of clear rose

54

pink. If faded blooms are removed immediately, you very often get another flush of flowers in early autumn.

Flowers and foliage are useful in fresh arrangements. The leaves can sometimes be glycerined in July. Flowers can be air dried or, for a better flower spike, dried in desiccant. Seed heads can be air dried, glycerined or preserved in anti-freeze.

Thalictrum delavayi (*T. dipterocarpum*, meadow rue) prefers well-drained moist soil, where the roots are not subjected to full sun. It grows up to 5 ft (1.5 m) and needs some support. The dainty, maidenhair fern-like foliage sets off the panicles of flowers, rosy lavender with yellow anthers, in summer. 'Hewitt's Double' has graceful sprays of rich lavender, double flowers.

Condition in the Savlon mix. Foliage can be glycerined in late July.

Veratrum do best in shady, moist conditions and in a sheltered position to protect the leaves from late frosts. They are an unusual alternative to hostas, with handsome pleated leaves appearing early in spring, pale green when young, darkening when mature. The flowers are like magnificent, frothy chandeliers, with hundreds of tiny star-shaped blooms on tall spikes in July.
V. album (false helleborine). Heads of creamy white and green flowers, height usually 4 ft (1.2 m). (See p. 56.)
V. nigrum. Plumes of purplish black flowers in a thick mass, reaching 3 ft (90 cm).

Stachys macrantha 'Superba'

The handsome foliage of *Veratrum album*

The leaves can be used almost as soon as they appear and, with careful dissecting, one stem will produce up to five hosta-type leaves. As the flowers are not very long-lasting, we prefer to leave them to go to seed, although we do remove a few small side stems to dry in desiccant. To dry the seed heads, cut the stems as soon as the seeds are set, stand them in 3 in. (7.5 cm) of water and allow to dry; alternatively you can stand them in one of the preserving solutions for one week, remove and hang upside down to dry. At Christmas time, the seed heads make delightful mock trees, sprayed with white paint and, while still tacky, sprinkled with glitter.

HARDY ANNUALS

We think it well worth devoting a little time to hardy annuals – so easy to grow, good for filling in spaces in the garden and, of course, useful for the arranger. Most annuals need all the sunshine they can get, so select an open position for them. The site should be prepared during the winter months by digging and incorporating garden compost if possible. However, do not make the soil too rich, as this will result in strong foliage growth at the expense of the flowers.

Sowing can usually start in early April. Just before this, spread bonemeal on the soil at the rate of 2 oz per sq. yd (67 g per m^2) and gently rake into the surface. If the soil is too wet, wait until conditions improve and then choose a quiet, still day for sowing. We believe the best way to sow is in shallow parallel drills, spacing these at roughly half the height of the plants [i.e. if the plants are 1 ft (30 cm) high, the distance between drills should be 6 in. (15 cm)]. Sowing in lines makes it much easier to distinguish between weeds and seeds in the earlier stages and the sooner the weeds are removed the better.

Thin the seedlings as soon as they are big enough to handle, in two or three operations if necessary. In dry weather, water the seedlings after thinning, using a watering can with a rose and gently watering along the drill; this will help to firm any seedlings that may have been loosened in the soil. The following list includes some of our favourites.

Atriplex hortensis 'Rubra'. Deep purplish red foliage and dock-like seed pods, to 6 ft (1.8 m) tall. Self-seeds very freely. The foliage can be used fresh. The seed pods are pale tan when glycerined.

Calendula officinalis (pot marigold). One of the most colourful and easily grown annuals, with blooms ranging from pale yellow to rich orange. 'Indian Ruler' is burnt orange with a mahogany centre. Height 1 ft (30 cm). The flowers are worth preserving in desiccant, to give you a warm rich colour for winter arrangements.

Centaurea cyanus (cornflower). Available in many colours, blue, mauve, pink, white, red and a new very dark maroon. Height 1–2½ ft (30–75 cm). Flowers can be air dried quite successfully, but better colours are obtained with desiccant.

Echium plantagineum (bugloss). Borage-like flowers in blue, pink, white or mauve, produced for many weeks, up to 1 ft (30 cm). Excellent as fresh cut flowers and can be dried in desiccant to give vibrant colours for winter use.

Lavatera trimestris. 'Mont Blanc' has pure white, mallow flowers appearing continuouly. 'Silver Cup' has soft pink flowers. An excellent garden plant, 2½ ft (75 cm) high. Very useful for large summer arrangements. Allow some of the stems to go to seed and glycerine them.

The pot marigold, 'Indian Prince' (left) and *Lavatera trimestris* 'Silver Cup' (right)

Lupinus 'Lulu'. Short-growing to 2 ft (60 cm) and very free flowering in many colours. Remove seed heads immediately to ensure continuous flowering. If a second sowing is made in June, they will flower well into the autumn. Good for cutting and will last a very long time if conditioned in the Savlon mix or by the starch method.

Nigella damascena (love-in-a-mist). Cornflower-like flowers in red, blue, mauve or white, followed by seed pods. Height 15 in. (38 cm). Flowers will dry successfully in desiccant (see p. 19). They can be air dried, but do not tie too many stems together as they tend to get caught up with each other. Either air dry the seed pods, or place them in the glycerine solution for four days, then remove and hang to dry.

Reseda odorata (mignonette). Grown for centuries for the fragrance of its rather undistinguished, yellowish white flowers on 1 ft (30 cm) stems. It is best to let these go to seed and then glycerine them. Leave in the preserving solution no longer than about ten days, tie in small bunches, hang up and allow to dry, when they will turn a beautiful cream.

Scabiosa atropurpurea (pincushion flower). A range of jewel-like colours, purple, almost black, red, mauve, pink and white. Height 1½–3 ft (45–90 cm). Long lasting as a cut flower and has very good seed pods.

Ornamental grasses

Ornamental grasses are of great value to the arranger, whether used fresh or dried or preserved in glycerine. Of the many annual varieties, the following are probably the most useful, all 1½–2 ft (45–60 cm) tall.

Briza maxima (quaking grass). Large nodding spikes.

Hordeum jubatum (squirrel's tail). Silky long-haired tassels.

Lagurus ovatus (hare's tail). Soft, creamy white plumes.

Setaria italica (foxtail millet). Nodding green heads.

Love-in-a-mist, *Nigella damascena*

Foxtail millet, *Setaria italica* (left) and everlasting flower, *Helichrysum bracteatum* (right)

To glycerine grasses, stand them in the solution for four days, remove, wrap carefully in newspaper, tie and hang in a dry, dark place for about one month.

Everlasting flowers

Helichrysum bracteatum (everlasting flower or straw flower). Large, brilliantly coloured, daisy flowers on plants 1–3 ft (30–90 cm) high. The blooms retain their colour well when dried and are probably the best-known dried flowers. It is advisable to take individual flowers as they open, rather than cutting the whole stem and sacrificing many buds. Cut when the outer petals have opened away from the centre, leave a 2 in. (5 cm) stem, insert a florist wire through the stem into the head of the flower and place upright in a jar in a cool place away from direct sunlight. They take about three weeks to dry.

Helipterum roseum. Daisy-like flowers in shades of white, pink or red. Height 1–1½ ft (30–45 cm). Cut flowers when just opening, tie in bunches and hang up as for normal air drying.

Scabiosa stellata (drumstick). Pale blue flowers which mature to bronze seed heads. Height 1¼ ft (45 cm). The seed pods can be air dried, but they last longer if given a drink of the glycerine solution for two days, before tying in small bunches and hanging to dry.

Xeranthemum annuum. Thin wiry stems to 2 ft (60 cm) carry paper-like semi-double, daisy flowers in rose pink, lilac or white. We find the best way to dry these is to pick them when fully open, stand in a container and put in a dark place. The flowers tend to close up as they dry, but a gentle steaming before use will quickly open them.

Design in flower arranging

Flower arranging is an art and there should be few hard and fast rules, but there are some basic principles which will help you on your way. The quicker you learn these, the more you will enjoy your arranging and gain confidence to improvise and create your own compositions.

A perfect flower arrangement should present a picture as a whole. You can choose a beautiful container and fill it with beautiful flowers, but unless the two are harmonious, the arrangement will finish as it began – container and flowers both beautiful but not making a whole picture. Try to select varied shapes and textures in your plant material and, if using many colours, a good balance of each, always remembering the suitability to the container.

There are various designs used in flower arranging, mostly based on geometrical shapes (see figure 7, p. 62). A good design will have all the following elements:

a) Proportion. Make sure the container is appropriate and of the right scale for the flowers and foliage. A good guideline is that the largest leaf or flower should not be more than one third the size of the container.

b) Balance. This will not only have the visual effect of equal weight and colour in the design, but it also means the practical aspect of an arrangement that will not topple over through being top-heavy or one sided.

c) Harmony. Everything, including the container, should be complementary and no single factor should dominate. Textures and shapes should be mixed with discretion to give interesting contrasts and the whole should have a sense of movement and rhythm.

Three types of plant form are used in every arrangement:

1 fine or pointed material, to create the outline shape;
2 medium or filler for strengthening the design;
3 large bold material for use at the base of the arrangement to give visual weight (see figure 6).

We will go through a basic triangle arrangement step by step. Select and prepare a container with your chosen method of mechanics, remembering that it is easier to do a mass arrange-

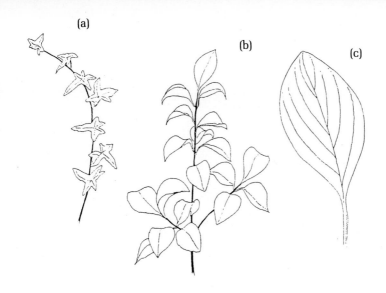

Figure 6: three types of plant material – (a) fine or pointed, (b) medium or filler, (c) large bold

ment in oasis or wire netting. Starting with the pointed material, put in the outline. The tallest point should be approximately one and half times the height of the container or one and a half times the width if it is a shallow container. The side placements should be long enough from point to point to measure approximately the same as the height. Using the rest of the pointed material, strengthen the first three placements. Make sure that you do not allow the stems to cross each other; they should all appear to spring from a central point.

We like to put in large leaves at this stage, bringing some over the edge of the container to soften the rim and give a three-dimensional effect. With your filler material, build up the design. Make sure you have some flowers or leaves overflowing the rim at the back to give further interest. Finally, the large bold material can be added, to fill in the centre. Round flowers are particularly good for this. Bring the flowers through the centre of the arrangement and cut each stem a little shorter than the previous one; this will give a softer effect and avoid having two heads at the same level. The last stem should be placed forward and over the rim of the container. (For illustration of a full triangle arrangement, see p. 16).

A Christmas arrangement (inverted crescent) – winter jasmine, holly and ivy (see also figure 8)

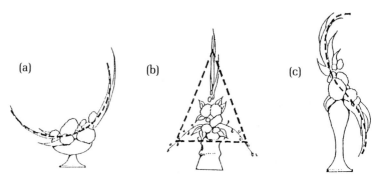

(a) (b) (c)

Figure 7: different arrangement shapes — (a) crescent, (b) triangle, (c) Hogarth curve

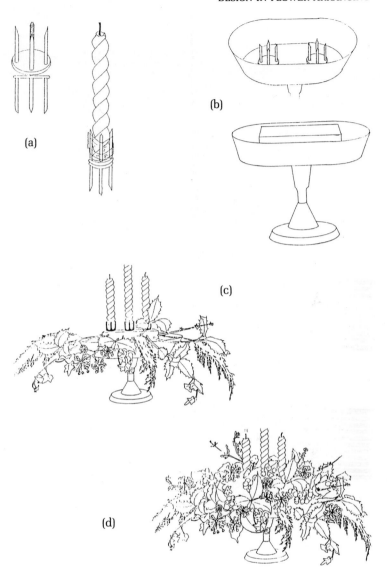

(a)

(b)

(c)

(d)

Figure 8: step-by-step Christmas arrangement (a) join oasis frogs with adhesive and place candles inside, fixing with tape; (b) put two more frogs in the container, secure them and place oasis on top; (c) insert candles in their frog holders in the oasis; determine size and outline of the arrangement with fine material, in this case *Cupressus macrocarpa* 'Goldcrest' and trails of small-leaved ivy; place a few ivy berries and short pieces of holly over the rim of the container to soften the effect; (d) complete the arrangement with sprays of winter jasmine and clusters of holly berries

Above: a New Year arrangement (assymetrical triangle) in a green urn
– *Garrya elliptica* catkins, witch hazel and hardy ferns, with foliage of
epimedium and variegated holly; it is effective for a long time, even
after the witch hazel blossom has dropped